T0030936

TRAILBLAZING WOMEN IN
SURFING

BY JEANNE MARIE FORD

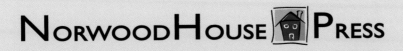

NORWOODHOUSE PRESS

Cover: Carissa Moore surfed in the Swatch Women's Pro Trestles competition in 2014.

Norwood House Press

For information regarding Norwood House Press, please visit our website at:
www.norwoodhousepress.com or call 866-565-2900.

Credits
Editor: Katharine Hale
Designer: Becky Daum
Fact Checker: Lillian Dondero

PHOTO CREDITS: Cover: © Mark Rightmire/The Orange County Register/AP Images; © Old Books Images/Alamy, 5; © Hawaii State Archives/Wikimedia Commons, 6; © Martin James Brannan/Fairfax Media/Getty Images, 9; © Richard Lyons/iStockphoto, 10; © Mark Rightmire/Orange County Register/AP Images, 13; © Martin James Brannan/Fairfax Media/Getty Images, 15; © Igor Meijer/DPPI/Alamy, 17; © Sorbis/Shutterstock Images, 20; © Igor Meijer/DPPI Lisa Andersen/Alamy, 21; © ZUMA/Alamy, 23; © Carol Cunningham/Vans Triple Crown of Surfing/AP Images, 24; © ZUMA/Alamy, 27; © Richard Milnes/Alamy, 28; © Pea Pop/Shutterstock Images, 31; © Epic Stock Media/Shutterstock Images, 33; © Louis Lotter Photography/Shutterstock Images, 34; © Francisco Seco/AP Images, 37; © Louis Lotter Photography/Shutterstock Images, 39; © Chris Rubino/Shutterstock Images, 41; © Francisco Seco/AP Images, 43; © Brandon Malone/Action Images/Reuters/Alamy, 45

Library of Congress Cataloging-in-Publication Data
Names: Ford, Jeanne Marie, 1971- author.
Title: Trailblazing women in surfing / by Jeanne Marie Ford.
Description: Chicago: Norwood House Press, 2023. | Series: Trailblazing female athletes | Includes bibliographical references and index. | Audience: Grades 4-6
Identifiers: LCCN 2022005091 (print) | LCCN 2022005092 (ebook) | ISBN 9781684507535 (hardcover) | ISBN 9781684048021 (paperback) | ISBN 9781684048083 (ebook)
Subjects: LCSH: Women surfers--Biography--Juvenile literature.
Classification: LCC GV837.9 .F67 2023 (print) | LCC GV837.9 (ebook) | DDC 797.3/2082--dc23/eng/20220209
LC record available at https://lccn.loc.gov/2022005091
LC ebook record available at https://lccn.loc.gov/2022005092

Hardcover ISBN: 978-1-68450-753-5
Paperback ISBN: 978-1-68404-802-1

353N—082022
Manufactured in the United States of America in North Mankato, Minnesota.

CONTENTS

HISTORY OF SURFING

No one knows exactly when the first surfers rode the waves. More than two thousand years ago, Polynesians took boards into the surf. After settling in Hawaii, some added a challenge. They stood on their boards and used their feet to steer across the water.

The ancient Hawaiian people had great respect for the ocean. They thought of surfing as an art, not a sport. It became an important part of their faith and culture. An ancient Hawaiian legend tells the story of Princess Kelea. She is remembered today for her love of surfing. The Polynesian word *wahine* means "woman" in the Maori language. It means "female surfer" in Hawaiian. Women, men,

The art of surfing has been practiced in Polynesia for millennia.

and children surfed together in Hawaii for hundreds of years. In the 1800s, Christian settlers came to the islands. They tried to forbid the traditions of hula dancing and surfing. For more than 50 years, Hawaiians continued to surf in secret.

Princess Ka'iulani was born in 1875. At 18, she was next in line to become queen of Hawaii. She fought to keep Hawaii

Princess Ka'iulani of Hawaii was a talented surfer. She fought for her nation's independence.

QUICK FACT

Mystery writer Agatha Christie was one of the first British surfers. Her writing helped introduce her readers to surfing.

an independent nation. Princess Ka'iulani ignored the settlers' rules against surfing. She bravely took her board into the waves. She died at 23 without ever becoming queen. But she breathed new life into surfing.

In the early 1900s, Duke Kahanamoku showed off his board skills on a world tour. The native Hawaiian introduced surfing to people across the globe. Surfing became a professional sport around 1960. It began with native Hawaiians of both genders. But white men quickly took over the sport. Women had to fight for their place in modern surfing history.

Margo Godfrey Oberg began competing in the 1960s. She was the first female professional surfer. Lisa Andersen brought strength and grace to the sport in the 1980s and 1990s. She was the first athlete sponsored by clothing company Roxy. Layne Beachley won a record seven world championships. Beachley is considered one of the greatest female surfers of all time. Stephanie Gilmore has also won seven world championships. She is known for her signature surfing style. Hawaiian Carissa Moore won the first Olympic gold medal in women's surfing in 2021. She follows in the footsteps of the first great *wahines*.

QUICK FACT

Surfing became more popular after World War II (1939–1945). The war led to improvements in making plastics. Surfers used the newly available materials to make surfboards faster and lighter.

CHAPTER ONE

MARGO GODFREY OBERG

Margo Godfrey was born in 1953 in Pennsylvania. Not long after, her family moved to Southern California. Godfrey began surfing. She entered her first contest when she was ten. She won against a group of 12-year-old boys. By the time she was 13, Godfrey was ranked as the fourth female surfer in the world.

The Rise of Women's Surfing

Like Godfrey, surfing was coming of age in the 1960s. The first world championship was held in 1964. In 1965, Joyce Hoffman won the women's title. Hoffman's power and style drew the attention of sponsors.

Margo Godfrey Oberg is considered one of the most important women in surfing history.

She appeared on the cover of *Life* magazine. Hoffman brought surfing into the mainstream. She became an inspiration for young female surfers. But female surfers were often ignored by the press. They faced **discrimination** from male surfers who didn't believe women should compete. Hoffman, Godfrey, and other female surfers had to earn respect through toughness and talent.

Surfers ride powerful waves called swells. Swells are caused by storms and wind. A wave needs to break, or crash, to be surfable.

Marge Calhoun

Marge Calhoun was born in 1924 in Los Angeles, California. She was a competitive swimmer and diver. She also worked as a movie stuntperson. After her husband gave her a board as a gift, she fell in love with surfing. In 1958, she went to Hawaii for a month. There, she became the first woman to win a surfing world championship. In 1961, Calhoun cofounded the United States Surfing Association. She was its first female judge.

In 1968, Godfrey beat Hoffman to win her first world championship. She was in ninth grade. The next year, Godfrey won every major event she could enter. She also became the first woman to earn money from surfing. People were calling her the next Joyce Hoffman.

By 1970, Godfrey had been dominating the sport for four years. But that was about to change. She took second place behind Sharron Weber at the world championship in Australia. Godfrey was crushed by her first defeat. She decided to take a break from competition. She hadn't even finished high school when she retired from surfing.

Retirement and Beyond

In 1972, Godfrey married Steve Oberg. Together they moved to a treehouse on the Hawaiian island of Kauai. She enjoyed Kauai's peacefulness. She also liked riding waves that were larger than California's. In 1975, clothing brand Lightning Bolt offered Margo Oberg a paid contract. She returned to surfing. Oberg and six other women competed in a major men's competition

Gidget

Kathy Kohner was a California girl who loved to surf. Her father wrote a novel called *Gidget*. It was about his daughter's surfing adventures. *Gidget* became a movie in 1959. It later became a television series. The popularity of *Gidget* inspired a generation of female surfers.

that year. Oberg ranked first out of the women and third overall. She beat out some of the best male surfers in the world. By 1981, she had won four world championships. It would take more than 15 years for another woman to beat her record.

In 1977, Oberg opened the Margo Oberg Surfing School. More than 40 years later, the school continued to operate on Kauai. Younger surfers strove to follow in Oberg's footsteps. They studied

Kathy "Gidget" Kohner (pictured) was inducted into the Surfing Walk of Fame as Woman of the Year in 2011. In 1995, Margo Oberg was the second-ever Woman of the Year inductee, after Joyce Hoffman in 1994.

her performances and treated her as a celebrity. She coached and encouraged the next generation of surfers. Oberg retired

There are two types of surfboards. Longboards float more easily. They're also more stable. Shortboards are harder to ride. But they give surfers more control.

from surfing again in 1991. She had ruled the sport for nearly three decades. She was inducted into the International Surfing Hall of Fame the same year. In 2000, *Sports Illustrated* included Oberg on its list of the top female athletes of the 1900s. Many consider her the most significant woman in the history of surfing.

Rell Sunn

Rell Sunn, a native Hawaiian, was born in 1950. Her hometown of Makaha, Oahu, had some of the biggest waves in Hawaii. She learned to surf from the greats. Duke Kahanamoku was one of her **mentors**. Sunn became Makaha's first female lifeguard in 1975. In 1979, she helped found the Women's Professional Surfing Association. She was diagnosed with cancer at age 32. At the time, she was ranked as the top surfer on the women's surf tour. Sunn continued to surf during her treatments. She died in 1998 at age 47.

Margo Godfrey Oberg won world championships in 1968, 1977, 1980, and 1981.

CHAPTER TWO

LISA ANDERSEN

Lisa Andersen learned to surf at age 13 near her Florida home. It took her weeks to learn to paddle out far enough to catch her first wave. When she finally did, she felt pure joy. She was instantly hooked on the sport.

Andersen's life at home was troubled. She had poor school attendance and grades. She spent time in juvenile detention for running away from home. Her parents blamed surfing for her problems. Her father grew so angry that he broke one of Andersen's surfboards. This act drove her to leave home for good at age 16.

Andersen bought a one-way plane ticket to Los Angeles, California. She slept on the streets of Huntington Beach at night. During the day, she entered surfing

Lisa Andersen was a successful surfer in the 1990s and early 2000s.

contests. She sent newspaper clippings to her parents to show them her success. Other surfers noticed her talent. They helped Andersen improve. She turned professional at age 17. In 1988, she was named **Rookie** of the Year.

Wipeouts, or falls from a surfboard, are a major danger for surfers. They can cause lasting injuries. Wipeouts can be deadly, especially in big wave surfing.

Surfer Mom

Andersen was known for her powerful moves and aggressive approach to waves. She consistently ranked among the top ten female surfers in the world. But she did not win a world championship in her first several years on the tour. In 1993, Andersen gave birth to her daughter. She was back on her board competing two weeks later. Andersen said her

Sofía Mulánovich

Sofía Mulánovich was the first Peruvian to compete on the World Surfing tour. In 2004, she became the first champion from South America. Lisa Andersen was her friend, mentor, and fellow competitor. Andersen said Mulánovich pushed her to be a better surfer. Mulánovich surfed professionally for 13 years. After retiring, she spent her time helping Peruvian kids learn how to surf.

daughter helped her focus on what she should be doing with her life. The next year, she won her first world championship. She won four in a row from 1994 to 1997. In 1996, she was the first female surfer in years to appear on the cover of *Surfer* magazine.

Andersen developed back problems after her daughter was born. In 1998, she left competitive surfing. That year, surfer Layne Beachley won her first world title. Andersen returned to the sport in 2000. Beachley's success motivated her to push herself harder. Beachley earned the world title that year. But Andersen was proud of edging out Beachley to win the last major competition of the year.

Andersen's son was born in 2001. She ended her professional surfing career for good. But she didn't stop surfing. And she soon found another way to make an impact.

QUICK FACT

Sea animals and plants such as kelp can cause serious injuries to surfers. Sharks may attack when they mistake surfers for prey. Surfers can get tangled in kelp.

Surfing Ambassador

Quiksilver founded Roxy in 1990. Now there are Roxy stores around the world.

Andersen was sponsored by Quiksilver in 1992. This company makes clothing for surfers and snowboarders. Andersen hated wearing a bikini while surfing. Sometimes bikinis fell off in the waves. Quiksilver let Andersen choose her own boy shorts from the company's warehouse. But the shorts weren't designed for women. Andersen worked with Roxy, the women's clothing line from Quiksilver. She helped design board shorts that were made to be comfortable for female athletes. In 1994, Andersen was the first athlete sponsored by Roxy.

Lisa Andersen came out on top in the 2000 Billabong Pro Final in Anglet, France.

In 2005, Andersen became Roxy's brand **ambassador**. She helped design new swimwear. She also became a coach and mentor to the athletes Roxy sponsored. She loved teaching and inspiring young surfers.

CHAPTER THREE

LAYNE BEACHLEY

Layne Beachley was born in Australia in 1972. She began surfing as a child with her father. She still remembers the excitement she felt the first time a wave rolled under her feet.

When Beachley was six, her mother died. Two years later, her father told her she was adopted. This was a confusing time for her. Surfing helped Beachley escape from her worries. The ocean was the place she went to feel safe.

Beachley was often the only female surfer on the beach. Whenever boys told her to leave, she ignored them. She learned to believe in herself. Beachley declared that someday she would be the world surfing champion. She was eight years old. The first time she competed in a surfing event as

Layne Beachley is a record-breaking surfer.

a teen, she came in last. She kept working. At 15, she finally won her first **amateur** competition.

Layne Beachley surfs in the 2004 Roxy Pro contest in Hawaii, part of the world championship tour.

Overcoming Challenges

Beachley turned professional at age 16. It took two years before she won her first pro event. A week later, she was diagnosed with chronic fatigue syndrome (CFS). She felt exhausted. She had to cut many foods from her diet. She had to take breaks from training. Beachley struggled with symptoms for years. She nearly quit surfing. CFS also caused her to experience depression. Beachley fought through her illnesses and continued competing. Surfing helped her heal.

Beachley faced other challenges. In 1995, she was ranked second in the world. But her sponsor, Quiksilver, paid her only $8,000 per year. She had to work four jobs so she could afford to keep surfing.

Maya Gabeira

Maya Gabeira grew up in Brazil. She watched the boys catching the biggest waves. Gabeira thought a woman should be doing the same thing. She decided to become that woman. In 2013, she nearly drowned after a surfing accident. She almost quit the sport due to her injuries. But she missed the thrill of surfing giant waves. In 2018, she set a Guinness World Record for the tallest wave ever surfed by a woman. In 2020, she broke her own record when she surfed a wave of 73.5 feet (22.4 meters).

Unlike some of her competitors, Beachley preferred tackling big waves. At Sunset Beach, Hawaii, she would sometimes enter the churning surf without a board. Then she would let the giant waves crash over her. She learned to control her fear. She came to enjoy the thrill. But she struggled in competitions with smaller swells. In the world championships, she finished second to Lisa Andersen twice. Beachley began to see Andersen as the one thing standing between her and her lifelong goal.

Beachley trained harder. When she faced off against Andersen in 1998 at Snapper Rocks, Australia, she finally won. Beachley was crowned world champion that year. She went on to win for six years straight. No other surfer had ever won six consecutive titles. Her record held strong more than a decade later. In 2006, she grabbed a seventh title.

Even at the top of her sport, Beachley never stopped pushing herself. New technology let surfers take on larger waves. Jet Skis could tow people out to swells they could not paddle to safely. This practice was called tow-in surfing. Beachley embraced it. In January 2001, she set a record for the largest wave ridden by a woman.

Layne Beachley won her seventh world championship in 2006.

Helping Others

After suffering a neck injury, Beachley retired from professional surfing in 2008. She had earned more money in her career than any female surfer before her. Beachley went on to start a clothing company. She also gave much of her time and

Since retiring from professional surfing, Layne Beachley spends her time teaching others about success and overcoming challenges.

energy to helping others. She started the Aim for the Stars Foundation. It provided money to help women and girls follow their dreams. In addition to her charity work, Beachley became a popular author and motivational speaker.

In 2018, Beachley competed in the first women's Azores Airlines World Masters Championship for surfers over 45. Twenty-five years after her first major victory, she added a new surfing title to her list of accomplishments.

World Masters Championship

The Azores Airlines World Masters Championship was held in 2018. Surfers over the age of 45 were invited to attend. The event had been held in 2011. But 2018 was the first year with a women's division. Layne Beachley competed against five other women. She went against Hawaii's Rochelle Ballard in the final to win the title. Some of the competitors had been fierce rivals in the 1990s. Many saw the event as a reunion.

CHAPTER FOUR

STEPHANIE GILMORE

Stephanie Gilmore was often called "Happy Gilmore" because of her joyful personality. Nothing made her smile more than the water. Gilmore was born in Australia in 1988. She began surfing at age ten and turned pro at 17. In 2005, Gilmore beat reigning world champion Layne Beachley in the Roxy Pro competition. She went on to win her first world title in 2007. She'd taken the day off from high school to compete.

Setbacks

In 2010, Gilmore was attacked outside her house. She suffered a broken wrist and a head injury. Gilmore had just won four world titles in a row. She hadn't been out of the water for more than a day in years. Now doctors told her she couldn't surf for six weeks. But her

Stephanie Gilmore is an Australian surfing champion.

next event was in six weeks. She felt impatient to return to training. She did so before her body was ready. At the next event, she felt so weak that she sat in the sand and cried. She realized she was not going to win the championship that season.

Some people thought Gilmore's career was over. Her confidence suffered. She realized that she had been too focused on trophies. She had lost her love of surfing. Gilmore began surfing for fun again. Soon, she got back on track. Later wins felt even more meaningful. She had worked harder to achieve them.

Gilmore's graceful style set her apart from her competitors. She tied Beachley's record with a seventh world championship in 2018. In a television interview, she thanked Beachley for the example she had set. Beachley texted and tweeted her congratulations, sharing Gilmore's joy.

Bethany Hamilton

Bethany Hamilton is a surfer from Hawaii. In 2003, she was attacked by a shark. She lost her left arm and nearly lost her life. She was 13. Less than a month later, she was back in the water. Surfing with one arm was hugely challenging. So was overcoming her fear of sharks. But her love for surfing was stronger. Two years after the attack, she won a national surfing championship.

Layne Beachley (in pink) hugs Stephanie Gilmore after a 2008 competition.

Beyond Surfing

Gilmore believed that surfing was about the relationship between the ocean and the surfer. She was committed to ocean **conservation**. She had seen the effects of pollution and trash in the ocean. She participated in a program started by surfers. It was called Take 3 for the Sea. Every time she

Stephanie Gilmore has fought for equality in the sport she loves.

went out to surf, she tried to pick up three pieces of trash. Gilmore also knew the amount of air travel she did for her career was bad for the environment. She tried to make up for that by making **sustainable** choices in her personal life.

She used refillable water bottles and plastic-free products whenever she could. She also drove an Audi electric car. Gilmore became a brand ambassador for Audi. Roxy also sponsored Gilmore. Like Lisa Andersen, she helped design swimwear for the company.

Sponsorships have always been important for female surfers. Gilmore often earned less for winning an event than a male competitor. Sometimes she earned four to five times less. She fought for pay equality between men and women in surfing. She also fought for access to equal conditions. Men often competed during peak wave conditions. If the wave quality declined, the women would be sent out to

Equal Pay

A group called the Committee for Equity in Women's Surfing, founded in 2016, fought for women to receive the same pay as men. In 2019, the World Surf League began offering equal pay in all surfing competitions. It was the first US-based worldwide sports league to give women the same prize money as men.

compete. Gilmore thought greater fairness in the sport would draw more women to competitive surfing. Surfers such as Beachley had fought to make Gilmore's path easier. Gilmore wanted to do the same for the next generation of female surfers.

QUICK FACT

There are two major surfing organizations: the International Surfing Association and the World Surf League. Both groups worked together to make sure every top surfer had a chance to qualify for the Tokyo Olympics.

Surfing was first added to the Olympic Games in Tokyo, Japan. They took place in 2021. Gilmore surfed for Australia. She was ranked fifth in the world. But she was knocked out in the third heat. She was disappointed by her result. But she loved the Olympic experience. Gilmore was already looking forward to the next Olympic Games.

Stephanie Gilmore competed in surfing's Olympic debut in 2021.

CHAPTER FIVE

CARISSA MOORE

Carissa Moore was born in Honolulu, Hawaii, in 1992. Her father taught her to surf before she started kindergarten. Moore's father is white. Moore's mother is part Native Hawaiian and part Filipina, raised by a Chinese American family. Carissa Moore felt a strong connection to the **diversity** of Hawaiian culture.

Moore's parents divorced when she was ten. Her father lived closer to the ocean. Surfing was a love Moore shared with him. When she was at her mother's house, she wrote him letters. She wanted to stay connected to surfing through him.

Surfing Star

By the time Moore was eight, many people had noticed her surfing skills. At age 12,

Moore discovered her love of surfing through her family and Hawaiian culture.

she talked to her father about turning pro. She won 11 tournaments before she started tenth grade. In 2008, at 16, she beat Layne Beachley in a Triple Crown of Surfing event in Hawaii. This is an event with three stages of competition. That made Moore the youngest surfer ever to claim the title.

Khadjou Sambe

Khadjou Sambe grew up in Senegal. She had never seen a Black female surfer. Her parents disapproved of the sport. She worked for years to persuade them to let her try it. Sambe screamed with happiness when she caught her first wave. She became Senegal's first female professional surfer. She also coached girls at a school called Black Girls Surf. She advised them not to listen to anyone who tells them they can't do something.

In 2010, Moore won $15,000 at a competition in New Zealand. She donated the entire amount to a charity that helped kids learn about the ocean. She was later named 2010 Rookie of the Year on the women's professional tour. In 2011, she won her first world title. She unseated four-time champion Stephanie Gilmore. At age 18, Moore became the youngest world champion on the tour.

QUICK FACT

During each round of a competition, surfers can ride as many waves as they wish. Judges look at factors such as difficulty, moves, speed, and flow. They combine the two best rides for a surfer's total score.

Carissa Moore catches air at a competition in California.

Later that year, she became the first woman to win a place in the Men's Triple Crown competition.

In 2012, Moore joined a group of Latin American surfers on a trip to Central America. They taught kids to surf and to respect the ocean. For the next several years, Moore and

Gilmore took turns at the top of the women's tour rankings. Moore won two more world championships in 2013 and 2015. In 2016, the mayor of Honolulu made January 4 Carissa Moore Day.

Fighting Back

After her early success, Moore found herself struggling with her fame. She battled anxiety and body image issues. She worked with a coach to tame her negative thoughts. She learned that what made her feel best was helping others. In 2018, Moore started a charity called Moore Aloha. Its goal was to bring young women together and **empower** them through surfing.

The year 2021 was a big one for Moore. In April, she landed the biggest aerial of her career. Aerial moves are done above the waves. They are common in the men's game. Surfers like Moore are bringing them to the women's competition. That summer, Moore earned the first Olympic gold medal in women's surfing. And she brought home her fifth world championship in the fall.

Carissa Moore became the first person to win an Olympic gold medal for surfing.

In surfing, Hawaii is often considered separate from the United States. Moore usually represents Hawaii. However, Moore was part of Team USA in the Olympics. While carrying the US flag, she wore a yellow plumeria flower behind her ear. Her mother had given it to her to remind Moore where she came from. Surfing was a Hawaiian sport. Moore was Hawaiian. Now she had brought home the sport's highest honor.

Amuro Tsuzuki

Amuro Tsuzuki grew up in Japan. The bay near her home produced small waves. She began traveling two hours to surf bigger swells. At age 11, she competed in her first surfing contest. In 2020, Tsuzuki became the first Japanese woman on the World Surf League Women's Championship Tour. In 2021, she competed in the Tokyo Olympics. She took home the Olympic bronze medal for Japan.

Layne Beachley (left) and Stephanie Gilmore compete in 2008. The trailblazers of women's surfing have built upon the successes of athletes before them.

Surfing began as an ancient Hawaiian practice of art and faith. Now it is a sport practiced around the world. Female surfers have fought hard to earn the same pay and respect as men. New technology lets today's surfers tackle bigger and more dangerous waves than before. Many changes have come to surfing over the centuries. But the joy and the thrill of riding the waves will always be at the heart of the sport.

GLOSSARY

amateur
an athlete who is not paid to compete in a sport

ambassador
a representative

conservation
stopping the waste of resources

discrimination
unfair treatment based on characteristics such as gender and race

diversity
including people of many different backgrounds

empower
to help someone gain confidence

mentors
teachers or advisers

rookie
someone in her or his first full season in a sports league

sustainable
done in a way that does not use a lot of natural resources and can be continued

FOR MORE INFORMATION

Books

Dwinell, Kim. *The Science of Surfing: A Surfside Girls Guide to the Ocean*. San Diego, CA: Top Shelf Productions, 2021.

MacDonald, Lisa Steele. *The Science of Waves and Surfboards.* Huntington Beach, CA: Teacher Created Materials, 2019.

Walsh, Jenni L. *Bethany Hamilton.* New York, NY: Scholastic, 2019.

Websites

Carissa Moore
(https://olympics.com/en/athletes/carissa-moore)

Visit Carissa Moore's official Olympic page to learn more about the athlete.

The Physics of Surfing
(https://ed.ted.com/lessons/the-physics-of-surfing-nick-pizzo)

How exactly does surfing work? Find out about the physics of surfing in this animation.

Surfing
(https://kids.britannica.com/kids/article/surfing/439473)

This website provides a brief introduction to the world of surfing.

INDEX

ABOUT THE AUTHOR

Jeanne Marie Ford is an Emmy-winning TV scriptwriter and holds an MFA in Writing for Children from Vermont College. She has written numerous children's books and articles and also teaches college English. She lives in Maryland with her husband and two children.